I0622794

The F Word

Why Failure Doesn't Mean Ruin

An Ignite and Inspire Series Book

Joy

MJP Publishing LLC

Copyright © 2023 by Joy, MJP Publishing LLC

All rights reserved.

Paperback ISBN 979-8-9875394-4-6

Ebook ISBN 979-8-9875394-5-3

No part of this book may be reproduced in any form or by any electronic or mechanical means, including information storage and retrieval systems, without written permission from the author, except for the use of brief quotations in a book review.

Legal Notice: This book is copyright protected. This book is only for personal use. You cannot amend, distribute, sell, use, quote or paraphrase any part, or the content within this book, without the consent of the author or publisher.

Disclaimer Notice: The information contained within this document is for educational and entertainment purposes only. All effort has been executed to present accurate, up to date, reliable, and complete information. No warranties of any kind are declared or implied. Readers acknowledge that the author is not engaging in the rendering of legal, financial, medical or professional advice.

By reading this document, the reader agrees that under no circumstances is the author responsible for any losses, direct or indirect, which are incurred as a result of the use of the information contained within this document.

To my friends who, through the years, handed me a towel and hot cup of tea when I fell face down in the mud. Your support, loyalty, and love helped keep me going so that I get to do what I do each day.
Thank you!

Sarah Knier, Wendi Schambach, Cheryle Thompson

Contents

Introduction

JR walked to the Toastmaster's lectern bright eyed and ready to make her first speech in front of the group. Her voice and hands trembled slightly as she started with a familiar question, "What would you do if you knew you couldn't fail". Then, she took the speech in a different direction than I thought, we probably all thought, she was going to go. JR went on to discuss making clothes and how she defines failure as it relates to that, and then took it further describing how she reduces her chances of failure by repurposing material and reusing patterns. She was wearing two visual aids, her cardigan (she *made* that!?) and her dress that was made out of an old tablecloth. The looks around the room spoke volumes, *no way*! We were so busy being amazed that she made those lovely pieces that we were surprised when she told us that each one represented, what started out to her, as a failure.

The word failure has been used in so many ways that we don't know if we are supposed to be motivated by it or scared of it. Is it good or is it bad? Do we embrace it or shun it? Is there a middle ground? Do we *Fail Forward, Chase Failure, Drift Into Failure, Triumph Through Failure,* see *The Gift of Failure, Anticipate Failure,* or have *A Love Affair with Failure?* These are just seven of hundreds of books on failure. So where do we start? Who do we listen to? What is the right answer?

This book examines the definition of failure, breaks down and puts the parts in perspective, looks at the different sides and shades of it, and teaches you how place "failure" where it belongs, on your terms, so that you are equipped to be in charge of your life and forward movement.

Each book in the Ignite and Inspire series is born from 20 years of mentoring and helping people. While you and I may not be face-to-face, you do have access to resources that I suggest for each book sorted by chapter on MsJoysPlace.com, as well as a Discussion Group. Bring your questions *and* your expertise. *Everyone has something to add.*

Take Note and What to Expect

- This book is for your personal life, not your business or non-profit. Although you can apply some of this information to those, this book is specific to you as an individual and not how to run a successful venture.

- There will be a lot of examples in this book to help visualize a concept. *Please do not let the simplicity of them bother you. A simple explanation makes it easier to learn a complex concept.* If you find yourself in a way worse situation than the simple example, please know that you can still apply the information to your situation. If you find yourself at a sticking point, look up the resources for this book on my website or reach out to the Discussion Group.

- Every book in this series is intentionally compact. All of the fluff is removed to get right to the heart of the matter. These books may be small, but they are dense with information, insight, and help. Their purpose is to help you see that you can, and get you headed in the right direction. Remember that *you will get out of it what you put into it.*

- You will need paper and something to write with (journal and pen, notepad and pencil, whatever it looks like for you). Go ahead and get those now. As you read, jot down things that come to mind, and also use it to answer the questions you come across as they apply to you or your situation. You will be glad that you tracked your journey!

Failure Analysis

Before diving into our examination of failure, let's set up a plan so that you can *learn as you go through the book.* We will start by looking at failure analysis.

As defined by sciencedirect.com "The failure analysis is a technical procedure to investigate the root cause of failure of a product, equipment, or an unintentional mistake in designing, manufacturing, or any unseen problem in a continuous process."

As defined by marketbusinessnews.com "Failure analysis involves investigating how something failed, why it failed, and how to prevent it from happening again. It is a systematic and logical examination of a machine or equipment."

As defined by corrosionpedia.com "Failure analysis is the systematic investigation of a part failure with the objectives of determining the root causes of failure and the corrective actions needed to prevent future failures. Failures occur when some system or part of a system fails to perform up to the expectations for which it was created."

_____

Site after site defines failure analysis pretty much the same way. While they are referring to objects, I proposed that you use this idea for yourself.

How? First, you will do basic analysis as you go through the book. Then you will take the ideas, lessons, and new perspectives with you and immediately apply these things as needed as you go through your days. If a bump or caution comes along, you will use the tools gained from reading and applying what you have learned in this book; and failure as you once saw it, will be a thing of the past.

1. As you read: Once you realize that a specific part applies to you, take a personal inventory. Don't just read through these pages and expect that *walla!* all is well with your world. You will need to put in effort to evaluate what is being said and match it up with your life to see if you need to make an adjustment. Take time to fully engage in the process of answering any questions and looking inward at what can be adjusted or applied before going to the next section.

2. As you go through life: Once you are done with this book, you will be more equipped to view "failure" in a different light. Having gained other viewpoints, your feelings toward it should be such that you feel empowered to really look at the situation and place it in a healthy and useful perspective. Do this each time you find yourself shifting back to an old pattern or thought process. Keep making the effort and it will quickly become second nature!

Good or Bad?

Good and bad is relative to a situation. They are morals that you assign based on your preconceived ideas and perceptions; reality as you see it at that moment in time. However, in this book, specifically toward the word "failure", I am not referring to the morals of good and evil, or speaking of religion or theology in any way. *I am strictly using the thought that "there is no good or bad" to frame how we should see something that didn't go right, or as some would phase it: a "failure".*

Why? Once we add a moral judgement to this word, we deepen the impact, positively or negatively. When we step back and view a familiar subject in a different way (removing any moral or emotion toward it), we can see it in a light that we may not have known could exist. We open ourselves to revelation and enlightenment that can untangle the emotions and connection to it that, in most cases, shackle us to concepts that can make us feel "less than" or "not good enough", slowly stripping away our self-esteem and eventually how we value ourselves. Then life gets darker and grimmer, slowly evaporating the creativity and enthusiasm with which we used to start a new skill or project. For the purpose of learning, we will stay neutral in our feelings toward failure in an effort to evaluate it in its various forms, and pull away from any emotional attachment or preconceived idea.

Since the concept 'there is no good and bad when we refer to the word failure' may be new to you, I will repeat and rephrase what I am saying because it is imperative that we start off on the right foot. I am not saying that good and evil do not exist. I am not saying that morals do not or should not exist. I am saying that in the case of this subject, failure, if we stay middle of the road, neutral, and assign no "good" or "bad" to it, we will be able to view it afresh and rewire our perceptions, thus increasing the daylight in our lives and bring back an excitement, adventure, and maybe even fun to trying new things or trying again at something we set aside or gave up on.

To sum up, while we are considering the various aspects of what is called failure, there is no good or bad. It just "is". At this time, place the word in neutral as best as you can so that as we go through the various topics relating to it, it will be easier for you to turn it over and examine all sides without reservation. If you feel yourself feel some type of way as a new topic is brought to light, let that be your clue to take a moment and breathe, shift your opinion of it into neutral, and read that section with an open mind. This is where change, healing, and growth happens.

I will continue to use the words "good" and "bad" throughout the book *for ease in explaining* complex and often interwoven concepts, subjects, and categories, as well as pointing out how the majority view a specific aspect of the word.

As with most subjects, "failure" does not fit neatly into any box; most often overflowing into and intermingling with other root sources, subjects, and thought processes. I have done my best to separate the subjects out so that we can examine them. As you read, keep in mind the web of thoughts and emotions, of past and present, that make up we humans.

Failing, and worse, feeling like a failure, is a miserable place to be. So, let's get on the road to removing its power over us by understanding how and why we see it as we do.

Chapter One

Your reality is as you perceive it to be. So,
it is true, that by altering our perception
we can alter our reality. ~ William
Constantine

To get started unpacking the various sides of failure, let's look at some of its synonyms.

Bomb

Break/Break Down

Decline

Deficient

Deteriorate

Disappointment

Fall/Fall Short

Flunk

Forfeit

Go Wrong

Insufficient

Lack of Success

Lose

Miss

Unsuccessful

Looking at these words, which make up the definitions of both fail and failure in the four dictionaries that I looked at, every time that I fell off of my bicycle, burnt the pizza, hit a pothole, had to pause at the landing and catch my breath before going up the next flight of stairs, shredded the wrong document, and received a rejection letter for an article submission; I failed. Well, I disagree and I bet that you do too.

You were probably thinking "bicycle: maybe you hit a rock", "pizza: you probably didn't hear the timer", "pothole: maybe the road was covered with leaves"... and you would be right. But the definitions, the synonyms, say that I failed.

So, how does a simple thing like burning the pizza cause one to feel as badly as those responsible for the space shuttle blowing up? Why would getting a rejection letter make one angrily rip it into tiny pieces as tears run down their face? The reasons are many and usually run deep, and we will be touching on most of them. Your job is to look honestly at each topic and see if that describes you, and then set about making the changes necessary to overcome that part so you can get to the place where a rejection letter makes you shrug while you submit the article somewhere else. It is then that you will have skills like what kept Walt Disney knocking on banker's doors over 300 times when the previous one laughed at his concept of a cartoon mouse.

You may be reading this in a jail cell, after your business or marriage collapsed, or other much more extreme scenarios. Trust me when I say that I have experienced *huge* "failures" too and even if I am not in your exact shoes, enough other people have been and have moved to a better scenario, that I know you can too!

This information is universal. It is not specific to nationality, gender, age, or any other exterior factor. We all have a different starting place. No, that isn't fair, but it is reality. So, let's just say that we are each at our own starting line and judge our progress based on *our own*, individual efforts.

Looking at the sampling of words again, it is easy to see why one would equate any 'it didn't go as planned' scenario with the word failure. I think that we can all agree that not *every* negative is a failure, just like the examples above. Yes, technically hitting the pothole was a failure as that word is defined, but was it really a failure on my part or can with give some allowance for the fact that the road was covered in leaves and no one could see that pothole? Could it simply just be an accident?

How do we know when something is a failure and when it isn't? And, how do we not go to the other extreme and excuse away true failures? Why do we feel so yuck inside when something has failed? Why are some people so flippant when they fail? Who gets to decide if this is a failure or not?

To begin answering these questions, we first need to set up some boundaries and get some perspective.

- Life is you vs you. Don't look at other people (unless you are truly trying to learn from the scenario). That is both sides: not being jealous of how they didn't fail (you aren't in their heart and head, so you don't really know), or judging them on how they did fail (that should need no explanation, but let's just say, keep your nose on your own face and run your own race). In the pothole example, I am chalking it up to an unfortunate accident. You are certainly allowed to see it as a failure on my part. *Ideally* you would have no opinion at all because it is my business and not yours. Do you see how circular all of this can become? So, go back to the main idea and the both sides comment. That will help you stay on a less cluttered path.

- Failure is subjective, meaning each person gets to define failure for their own self and their own life. As you grow, your personal definition will grow too. *Start where you are.* There was a time when I would have beat myself up over that pothole incident. Decades and many lessons later, that situation doesn't have the same definition (or negative impact on me) as it did all those years ago. As you apply the principles in this book, you will experience that type of growth as well.

- Like all subjects, failure is a web of everything from childhood programming to how you understand how the task at hand is supposed to be performed, and so much more. As you read, look at the point being made along with the bigger picture, and apply that to your life. Also, take advantage of the resources provided for you. They should clear up any confusion and help you grow exponentially.

When you believe that you have failed, you could experience a variety of emotions such as anxiety, sadness, and embarrassment. Instead of going into each of these and other things you could feel as a result of a perceived failure, let's shed some light on why you are afraid of what is perceived as failure, as well as your perception of failure as a whole. This will help you understand it better, which will give those feelings less, or even no hold on you.

Chapter Two

**Fear makes the wolf bigger than he is. ~
German Proverb**

ortunately, most of our reasons for hating
failure so much is fear based. I say fortu-
nately because when you fix one thing, you
have fixed most. That sounds like a good trade off to
me! So we will start by looking at how fear shows up
in various forms and many ways humans react to it.
I'll begin with a personal journal entry. It references
a scenario that was the beginning of moving my life
onto its current course. (I tracked down that entry
and put it first so that the story is easier to follow.)

September 2010

*I was helping Sharon organize her
home office and saw a magnet on the*

filing cabinet across the room. It was a simple black and white rectangle that had a question on it that caused me to pause. It asked simply: "What would you attempt to do if you knew that you could not fail?" The white letters popping off of the black background beckoned and I walked to the filing cabinet and just stared at the letters.

The word "fail" had my attention immediately. I loathe that word as it has been my companion too many times in life, other times taunting me from the shadows, always there, lurking, ready to pounce.

Wanting to shake myself free from that word and all that it means, I read the question again and it challenged me: "So, you gonna get moving on all those dreams that you have put on hold? Do you even want to attempt something or are you chicken?" As I let my eyes move up the wall and to the ceiling looking at nothing in particular, my thoughts continued accusing me: "You are afraid to fail". I let my eyes go back to that powerful question. Reading it again it asked me in a soothing way: "Can you let yourself see no-fail"? I am not sure which thought had the biggest impact, but that does not change the fact that I was moved.

August 2016

That was nearly 6 years ago!!! A lot of life has happened since then and this once recovering perfectionist is now recovered with lots of little successes under her belt!

Life has handed me varying quantities of lemons since that day in 2010, but that hasn't stopped me. At times, I have had to get real with myself and re-start my plans, but since that day in Sharon's office, I have never been the same. Most, if not all that is being shared in this book, I have had to overcome and learn as I went through things. Later I used these lessons to help others and they too saw results. Years later, so many have had success, I know that this information is worth sharing. At the bare minimum, it will at least get you well headed in the right direction.

As you read through each subject, realize how fear is the root cause, so that you don't magnify it when you encounter it again. Meaning, don't give into it, don't feed that wolf, and it will lose its hold on you. Jack Canfield put it quite well saying, "Everything you want is on the other side of fear."

Control and Perfectionism

Do you have to control how everything is done? Does everything have to be perfect? Is it your way or the highway? Are those around you slightly more miserable because the hand towel or toilet paper was hung backward of your standard? Did getting the blue toothbrush instead of the purple one really ruin your day? *Do you think that if everything is perfect and you are in full control that you have ensured that you will not experience failure?*

When you are afraid to "mess up" you will hold on so tightly and require so much perfection (not just of yourself but usually those around you too) that you will lack quality relationships at home, socially, and at work, and will be miserable in the process. This type of person is ever waiting for the other shoe to drop, and stays in a constant state of stress knowing that at any minute the report won't be accepted, the cookies will be slightly over done, and the parent/teacher/boss will find fault with *something*.

I remember cleaning the already clean house to utter perfection in anticipation of my mother-in-law coming to visit for the first time in my then 17 years of marriage. I even vacuumed the ceilings! The morning that she walked into my house, she walked right to a spider web that must have appeared overnight right above the sliding glass door. I was so mortified that when I would recount that story, even *years* after the incident, my cheeks flushed. Today I just laugh. Who cares?

Fast forward a few years from then. I was working at an auto-parts store and by then I had started to realize that perfectionism was bondage, always keeping me on edge. That day was a game changer for me!

I was putting away the shipment and my boss came over to find out what was taking so long. I waved my hand like Vanna White, down the aisle so that he could see how perfect each and every row was. It was a sight to behold, I tell ya! He rolled his eyes and walked away. One of my co-workers shouldered up to me, knowing I was confused, and told me that it usually takes about three hours to put away the whole truck and I had only touched one aisle in that time. I thanked him and started shelving things where they went making sure that the labels were generally front facing and had the rest of the stock put away in no time. I realized that day that *sometimes good enough is good enough.* What I learned over time is that good enough is defined by the value that you put on something or its importance in the grander scheme.

Back then, I was still proofreading books regularly. For those, good enough was *not* good enough. They warranted my perfection touch. I started applying the store shelving idea to my personal life in little ways with my pantry being the biggest eye opener. While I didn't have the satisfaction of a perfectly aligned and organized pantry, everything was put away in a way that made sense and could be found quickly, *and I hadn't spent untold amounts of time moving things around to make it "perfect".* It sounds so silly now, but back then, I wanted to control anything that was possibly in my realm of control *because then it could never be accused of being anything less than the best.* What bondage! To have your self-esteem so wrapped up in how perfect your bathroom cabinets were organized or how straight everything was?

It's *Your* Turn

If you find yourself identifying with this, start looking for places where you are over controlling or expect perfection, and ask yourself if, in this case, can good enough be good enough? This will be different for each person. A chef may make sure that dishes served at home are as lovely in presentation as at the restaurant; whereas you and I may just plop the food onto the plate and head over to the table. For us, that's good enough, and for the chef it is not, and that is ok.

The goal here is to realize that *you cannot control and be perfect enough to avoid things not going right.* And that is also not failure. Just like the spiderweb that showed up overnight, stuff happens. Period. It didn't appear because I hadn't made an effort. It was a simple fact of life and no attempt at controlling the situation or trying to present my home as perfect 1) would work every time and 2) did not decide my value as a human, and should not have (had) any impact on how I saw myself as a homemaker, wife, daughter-in-law... person. Since that time, you will hear me say to someone who is apologizing for being less than the ideal or not reaching the mark of ultimate amazingness, "Tell you what, once I have reached perfection then I will expect that of you too." That is where I give them a gentle smile and we both know that means everything is ok, and your effort is appreciated right where it is.

Take some time to review this past month and look for patterns of control and/or perfectionism, then start asking yourself where or how you can apply "good enough is good enough". If your heart races at that very idea, it is ok. Decide that you will not be bound up like that any longer and start small, just like I did with the pantry. My heart was racing like a prize-winning horse the whole time I rearranged it. However, when I stepped back and saw that it still functioned well and I wasn't obsessed, anxious and miserable, it was worth going through the heart racing change. Over time I took on larger and larger things, not expecting myself to be the definition of perfection, and you know what? I began to laugh more, smile more, dance more, and even shrug more. *And people are more comfortable around me.* "I" am more comfortable around me!

Now it is your turn. Continue to read this book as you practice, as there are other areas discussed that can help you with this part too.

Being Lazy

Laziness is the other side of perfectionism and control. In this case, instead of being so afraid to fail that you go overboard, you are paralyzed by the fear so you do basically nothing. The person who identifies with this is so "over" feeling yuck at perceived failure ,or not being good enough, or not getting it right that they simply don't even try anymore. "Why bother" is generally the thought process and words escaping their lips.

This is not to be confused with true laziness or being a sloppy person. If you put the dish in the sink instead of rinsing and putting it in the dishwasher because you just don't want to expend the five second effort, you are lazy and this section doesn't apply to you. If you don't load it because a controlling/perfectionist will admonish you for having it placed in the wrong spot or the wrong direction, that is a fear of failure and within the scope of this book.

If this is you, you have options.

- Are you assuming that that is how you will be responded to? Be honest in your evaluation and response. If you have no history or evidence to back it up, it is probably an incorrect assumption.

- If you truly believe that is the response you will receive, can you let the person know that you'd like to help out more, could they show you how they would like it done (which will at the minimum add more peace into your life)? While in the learning process, genuinely ask for their thought process on why they do it that way if it is something that you see another way to do it. It is possible that this could be the beginning of their moment of realization and change. Make sure to remind this person politely that you are learning and to please be patient as you try. You can apply this to other scenarios at school or the job.

- If you find yourself not trying, not making an effort, "why even bother", take some time right now to trace back why.

What makes you freeze up or not even care your way to inaction? What is broken that you can fix? What questions can you ask or help can you get to overcome this issue?

- Keep reading as there are suggestions in other sections that can help with this too.

Procrastination

Stop saying you are planning and start doing. As W. Clement Stone said, "I think there is something more important than believing. Action! The world is full of dreamers. There aren't enough who will move ahead and begin to take concrete steps to actualize their vision."

Like laziness, this person doesn't take action. Why do people procrastinate? One reason is that if you don't do it, if you are forever planning or researching, if you are always looking for the best option, you think you are moving forward, but really you are avoiding the possibility of messing it up. If you think that you have a good reason for not doing it ("I'm going to research some other options", "I'm going to learn a little more about the process", "I don't know that I have all of the pieces just yet") then you prolong the potential for failure and all of the emotional baggage it carries along.

Once you have some education on the subject, make a plan and get going. You can always tweak it later, but at least get started.

Rejection

You will continue to learn about procrastination as this story begins with procrastination and then moves to the fear of rejection. (Remember, we cannot put life, emotions, intentions, etc in a neat little box. We are a living "domino effect".)

My friend went through a bad divorce which led to not seeing his daughter. Years after, he found her and through some almost miraculous events he was standing outside of the restaurant that she was in. But he was so paralyzed by the fear of failing to make an impression on her that he did nothing. He walked away. Literally. He turned around, got back in his car and left, after all of those years looking for her, paying for a private detective, etc. He was miraculously given another chance and found himself face-to-face with her and not only did she recognize him, she stood there waiting for him to approach her when she could have easily turned away or walked past him.

Instead of running to and hugging her like he had imagined himself doing over and over, he waved as he said hi and walked right past her like she was an acquaintance or neighbor, not his precious daughter that he fought to find and dreamed of having in his life once more. He was so afraid that she would not receive him, that he wouldn't know exactly how to phrase his feelings, that he did have as he put it "a guarantee that this is the right way to approach her", that he was willing to let her slip through his fingers again. Heartbreaking. But how many times have you done that? Not gone to the try out or applied for the promotion because you didn't want to hear, "no"? How many times did you make the excuse that you needed to practice a little more first (or something like that)?

Probably the main reason that one fears rejection is because it runs deep into the core of our being. The fullness of this subject is beyond the scope of this book, but let's touch on why it is so powerful and get pointed in a different direction.

Rejection questions the deepest part of you: your value or worth, your place or standing, your identity, and sometimes even your reason for getting up each day. This is why it is one of the most cutting emotions one can experience. Sadly, most people have experienced rejection in some form in their life. (Didn't make or got excluded from the team/ choir/ club/ fraternity, etc), she said no when you asked her to the prom, a parent or significant other removing themselves from your life, being fired or laid off, your best friend choosing another, some even see a loved one dying as a rejection.)

To make matters more complicated, what may make one person want to hide in a closet or eat a whole carton of ice cream in one sitting, would make someone else shrug their shoulders and move on to the next thing. The less impactful version is what we are aiming for in this book. I am not suggesting being hard hearted, but learning how to keep its impact to a minimum. Here are a few things to consider to get you started:

- Are you assigning your personal value to this event? If so, see yourself outside of it and assign value to *that* version of you.

- Lean into it, feel it, acknowledge that it is real and let it go just as fully as you might see a balloon deflating. If it comes back up, do it again. If it comes too often, once you realistically should have gotten past it, see the next point.

- Don't keep replaying it in your mind. Push stop on the repeat button by listening to or watching something that makes you laugh, motivates, and/or encourages you; move your body (even just a walk around the block can start to clear the mind); sing even if you don't feel like it, you can start with humming which has been proven to relax you; think about other things that are opposite of the reason for rejection or how the situation is wanting you to feel; ask a friend to help you see a better side of this situation.

- Be kind to yourself. In most cases, you didn't ask for this so don't be your own worst enemy.

If you find that rejection debilitates you, you should consider talking with a counselor to help you through it. Also, please look at the resources section of the website and spend some time working through it. Get a start on the recovery and then head back here and continue working on your perception of failure at the same time. Don't get caught in the perfection trap of "I have to have this subject completely under my belt before I can learn more". No. Life is a learn as you go gig. As someone once said, there is no dress rehearsal. Just keep picking up new things and get them working in your life, and you will find that over here you have obtained a new skill, and over here you are still slipping around like a baby moose on ice, and over here you are really starting to understand a concept and see how to work it into your life – simultaneously.

To wrap up the sections on procrastination and rejection, I'll take you back to my friend. Yes, it is very possible that his daughter could have rebuffed his efforts. But it is *also* possible to that she would have appreciated *any* effort on his part no matter how wobble-legged it came across. Years have gone by as he stands there undecided on how to reach out to her in a way that guarantees he won't fail.

Sometimes life gets dirty and you have to take risks or you will risk failure by default. Don't let that be you. Keep reading because we will touch on some of this in other sections. In the meantime, remember, just the *act* of moving in the right direction can provide movement juice. Start the car, take a deep breath, put it in gear, exhale, and go. It's scary. I know. I've lived it over and over again and come out better each time. *And you can too.*

Not Good Enough and Self-Sabotage

As I was growing up and learning as all children do, when things went sideways, I was called out and mocked by some of the adults in my life. When I didn't tie my shoes well, the laces loosened and I tripped over them and fell. I was told it was my fault for being so stupid. That will make an impression on a little one. By my early teens, I had learned that tears were defined as weakness dripping from your eyes, and worse, were a beacon, summoning the mockers to circle and laugh like hyena preparing to pounce on their prey. It was almost as though any perceived failure justified torturous taunting and put downs from those who's job it was to teach and protect me.

With comments from the adults speaking into my impressionable young self that I was such a screw up, I became increasingly harder on myself and even more fearful of the trouble I'd be in or surprisingly worse, the ridicule that would be slung without mercy should I not reach the ever-changing standard. I could not grasp the elusive carrot no matter how closely I followed directions, or how hard I scrubbed, studied, polished, combed... tried. I had such truly high hopes for myself, yet such a fragile ego; and the value that I saw in myself was sheer thin, easily torn with something as little as a mocking smirk by the adults. I clearly remember the second quarter in seventh grade crying so hard at the (all A's and) one B, that my homeroom teacher, Mr. Davis, kept me in that room for the whole next period until I could compose myself. I was so distraught because I couldn't bare the ridicule that I would get when the adults saw that report card. It was so bad that I would rather throw away a second-place ribbon than bring it home because it meant more comments and grinding on my almost non-existent self-esteem. No *wonder* I became a perfectionist and felt the need to control everything within my reach!

Feeling as though you are not good (or worthy) enough and its oft unrealized sidekick, self-sabotage, is the subject of many sad songs, self-help books, and the theme in way too many lives. I am positive that most of this book's readers nodded along in full, experiential understanding of my "the adults" stories. If you find yourself fearing failure because you don't think that you are good enough, if you find that you seem to be your own worst enemy and you don't even know why, it's time to lay that giant lie out!

To start, you can simply choose to go against your natural inclination to shy away from whatever it is you are afraid to fail at. Yes, that takes courage. Step up to the plate and swing. Did you miss? Try again. Miss again? Then swing again. You are learning, you are growing, you are trying, you are putting yourself out there when other people are sitting on the couch watching the next season of some show. It is ok to be proud of yourself for exhibiting courage, because few people do.

Let's look at this in very simple terms. If you keep swinging, what will you have to show for it? At worst, some lessons learned, experience under your belt, and a bit of confidence because you chested up to that giant lie. (The next chapter will help with this part of mind renewal.) Best case you hit a home run. It's a win-win. So put down the remote and pick up the bat. You may have to do this facing your giant lie multiple times before you start to untie the lie that the awful programming of 'I am not good (or worthy) enough' you have lived by for so long. Just keep at it.

If you still struggle after some real tries or you want to go deeper into healing and fully get rid of self-sabotage tendencies, look at the resources section for this book and consider visiting with a counselor who can help you work through it once and for all.

What is self-sabotage? It is little things that you do that cause you to fail and you most likely don't even realize you are doing it. Many of these little things are found in sections discussed in this book. For example: not putting it all out there because somewhere in the back of your mind you know (are programmed to think) you won't do well anyway so no need to really go all in; being paralyzed to inaction because the last time you didn't do it right; over analyzing or over preparing to avoid the step needed to move the situation forward so that you don't even have the chance to fail; and more. As you overcome the first issue and work on other areas in the various fear-failure causes, that by-product of self-sabotage will dwindle in your life and possibly leave forever.

Once you get past this issue or at least well on your way to overcoming it, then you will experience #28 from Benjamin Hardy's *31 Things That Will Happen When You Finally Decide to Live Your Dreams*: "You'd rather accept the consequences of trying your best than hiding your talents." I am excited for you to get there. Start today!

The Dark Room Syndrome

Most people will agree that it is scary to walk where you never have, or do something you've never done. What I call the "dark room syndrome" is when you are asking *where's the light, the path?* The unknown is usually not a source of excitement for most  people. The easiest way to turn on the light is to educate yourself, even if briefly, about what you are going to walk in to so that it is less scary. That greatly reduces your concern of failure because now you have an idea of what it looks like. How often have you gone through or done something and afterward you were like, *that wasn't so bad.* How does that apply to failure? Well, if you are doing something that you have never done before, chances are, you aren't going to initially be that great at it. Oh no, failure! * faint *. No. It means you attempted something you never have before and it was nerve wracking, but now the light is on! Now you have some experience and you can do a whole lot with some experience.

What did you gain from the experience? First, you took some time to read about that hiking trail that you had never been to so you learned something, secondly, you got the gear and made the trek. Good for you! Oh, you only made it a quarter of a mile in to the four-mile hike? And? Oh, were you expecting me to call you and your effort a failure? Sorry, you're looking at the wrong person for that. I am so proud that you made the effort, took the next step, got out of your comfort zone, and had the experience! Now, take what you learned and go do it again, better this time.

After you have done something for the first time, the light is on, you see the path, and it is no longer something you image, but something you have done. *Taking it from theory to tangible is powerful!* You now have perspective and should you choose to try it again, you know what to adjust for the next time around. After my first rock wall climb, I realized that I needed something to keep my hands from being sweaty. Then I learned about chalk! Very quickly, climbing no longer started with me standing on the floor looking way up at all of those colored plastic parts ("rocks") with uneasiness growing inside, but instead looking for the best path for my plump body, strong legs, short arms, and small hands. The path that worked for the ripped, 6'3" guy would not be the best path for me because he had length and strength that I did not. *I would not have known that my first go around.* Had I tried to do what he did, I would not have had a good experience because I was trying to live his experience, not my own. With each climb I gained more perspective and my confidence grew quickly. This simple example applies to all new ventures.

When I wanted to publish my first book, I spent approximately ten hours a day for six days learning everything that I could about the steps and process of self-publishing before I put it out there. I knew then and know now that that book isn't perfect. The cover is slightly off, the first few books printed had two typos on the back cover (how did I miss that?? – they have been fixed) and so on. But I learned so much in the *doing* of the process and *so proud of myself* for taking what I had learned and applying it. I learned even more when I published the second book and now, with my third book underway, I am not even nervous about the steps that I have taken twice before. And the best part is, I am starting to see places where I can do things better, because now I have perspective. I've turned on the light and continue to refine my path. Thinking of it like that, how can that first book be a failure?

Remember, the first time is a "walk through" to get the lay of the land and better understand what you are stepping in to. It is just a theory in your mind. Once you have actually stepped through it, like me with publishing that first book, it isn't as scary and then you start seeing it everywhere and answers to your questions start to come. And as a bonus, if you see it as an adventure, it is fun! So how do you do this? Let's recap:

- Seek out someone who has gone before you. My sister was my guide into the climbing world. She gave me some general tips then let me have an initial experience. After my first climb, I gave her some feedback (ex: my hands were sweaty and I had to keep wiping them on my pants which made me loose momentum) and she gave me suggestions. I was learning based on *my* experience, not on her experience or what I read in a book (not that those do not have value, as they do!). I walked my own path and did it myself. It took the tutorial I was given before my first climb, as well as the stories that she told me about her first few times climbing, from a mental understanding to a tangible experience, because now my own hands touched the rocks, and my own legs propelled me upward.

- Educate yourself to get some visibility on whatever it is that you are after and then just do it. You can read a book, watch videos, listen to podcasts, or take a class. Once you know what you are getting into it is less scary because at least the light is on and you can see where you are stepping; and once you do it, you have stepped and fear begins to dissipate. You may even find you like it! I dedicated 60 hours to learning how to self publish. That wasn't enough to be perfect, but I had plenty to get started and it made the whole process significantly more visible!

- Once you have your hands dirty, do a failure analysis and go again. If needed, further educate yourself enough to answer some questions and put the information to the test. Just like the climbing feedback and application, and realizing some errors made after my first *and* second books were out, I learned more, nodded my head as I made note, and kept on going. Keep tweaking the process for the next time around as needed. That isn't failure. It is learning; just like riding a bicycle.

Now that we have gone through many of the ways fear shows up either as a failure, causing us to fail, or see it as a failure, we can move on to other reasons why one may experience perceived or real failure.

Chapter Three

It is impossible to live without failing at something, unless you live so cautiously that you might as well not have lived at all, in which case you have failed by default. ~ J.K. Rowling

Sometimes we call something a failure that really isn't that at all, therefore take on the emotional consequences unnecessarily. Equally, there are times when we set ourselves up for failure unintentionally because, at it has been said "you don't know what you don't know". This chapter will shed light on both so that you can reframe situations and set yourself up for more favorable outcomes going forward.

If you see yourself in any of the following, take the time, right then, to evaluate it, and if needed, look up some resources to help you overcome it. Many times, it is as simple as you didn't realize that was the thing that was holding you back, and you can make an immediate adjustment to continue moving forward or try again.

A Mistake is Not a Failure and Falling is Not Failing

Mistakes are proof that you are trying (author unknown). That's pretty straightforward, but it may not be enough to handle the misconception that making a mistake is equal to failure, so let's look closer at it.

A stumble is not a loss.

Jesse Duplantis

A mistake is something that happened in the process of "go"-ing and "do"-ing. It is admirable that you are willing to get messy while other people watch (and miss out on the experience). Let them stand there in their insecurities. You just go right ahead and jump in that mud puddle! I believe that we all mentally know that there is a difference between failure and a mistake. So why does it still feel like a failure?

To clarify, I am not referring to an intentional

disregard for the obvious or for instruction. That is just asking for trouble. However, if you aren't aware of every factor (who is?), but doing your best to make it happen anyway, a mistake will probably be made. It isn't for lack of heart or trying, which are to be commended and can be built upon. Let's look at what Napoleon Hill had to say about this:

Failure is not a disgrace if you have sincerely done your best. We live in a competitive world that measures success by winners and losers, and insists that every victory creates a loss of equal dimension. If one person wins, it seems logical that someone else must lose. In reality, the only competition that matters is the one in which you compete with yourself. When your standard of performance is based upon being the best you can be — for yourself — you will never lose. You will only improve. Make it a practice to objectively review your performance from time to time. When you fall short, assess the situation and ask yourself: "Is there anything I would or could have done to change the outcome?" If the answer is "no," if you are satisfied that you've done your best, don't waste time reliving the past. Simply learn what you can from the experience, and then get into action again. If you consistently do your best, your temporary failures will take care of themselves.

There is also the argument that 'I knew better, therefore it was a failure'. This is a fine line. When we are talking about the pizza being burnt because I didn't take the timer with me to the other room and got involved in a phone conversation, how much of that is just a life happened mistake and how much an all out failure? Ultimately you decide for yourself. For me, it was a mistake and a lesson learned. I know that when I get on the phone that I give my attention to that person and will not hear something like a timer going off in the other room. Going forward, I will take the timer with me. Be kind to yourself.

Doing Your Very Best

Thinking back to what Mr. Hill said moves us right to the next subject, leading me to ask, did you leave it all on the field? Did you give your very best all the way to the final buzzer? Sometimes the game isn't won until the ball is in the air seconds before the buzzer then "swish"! Fight hard all the way to the end. Don't hold anything back. Don't quit even one second before it is over. You should be in full motion as the bell sounds, only then slowing your stride. Think back to last second won games, the last day sales pitch that sold, the last-minute submission that was accepted and won. Give it your all. Every second, *even the very last one*, counts.

There is a part two here. Who decides if it is your best effort? You do. Only you know if your heart was in it until the end. If someone wants to give their perspective of your performance, consider listening, because they may have some constructive feedback. But in the end, *it is what you believe that you did in those moments that decides if it was or was not your very best.*

That doesn't mean in a year you can look back at what you did today and beat yourself up over how you didn't do well. Because your best today will probably not be your best after you have practiced for a year. Your focus should be on evaluating your today; your effort right now. Let yesterday be what yesterday was and let tomorrow hold its own lessons and victories.

Keep in mind that in some areas, on some days in the same season, your best may shift. *And that is ok**. There may be times when you cannot lift as heavy as you did in a previous workout. That is ok*. You may not have presented the PowerPoint as effectively as you did last month. That is ok*. The essay may have been returned to you with a C+ written on top when all semester you have seen a B or better. That is ok*.

*As long as in that moment **you did** *your* best.

You Don't Want it Badly Enough

One way you may be unintentionally setting yourself up for failure is to by taking on the dream or goal without the commitment. Most people want the benefit of the work: the trim body, happy relationships, great career, but aren't willing to do what it takes to get there. If you aren't committed to seeing something through, with a best effort (not perfect effort because that doesn't exist), then you are preparing yourself to fail.

If you do really want it, alter your path to the goal that you can make happen. For example, you may not be willing to work out six days a week as well as completely change your eating habits all seven days in the week, but you really want the healthy body. What part of that do you want badly enough to make it happen? Maybe you can definitely work out two days a week and eat quality food during the work week. Great, then start there, get some victory and high fives under your belt, and then reevaluate. *Start where you are.* As we discussed earlier, don't wait for everything to be perfect. Just get going and adjust and get better as you go. Time is passing anyway so you might as well have some progress, lessons learned, lights turned on, and perspective shifts happening while the clock ticks.

There Isn't a Plan

If you have not heard this phrase before, you've heard it now: *If you fail to plan, you plan to fail.* As Brian Tracy said, "A clear vision, backed by definite plans, gives you a tremendous feeling of confidence and personal power."

A clear vision...backed by definite plans... Do you have a plan? By now you know that I am a huge proponent of get going, move, get your hands dirty. However, that assumes that you have done some research and at least some planning. There is a difference between jumping out with no idea or clue, and jumping out with at least a general plan in place. You need a starting point and a plan gives that to you. If you hit a bump, learn, grow, pivot, and keep working your plan, refining and adjusting it as you go. That is how to live this 'no dress rehearsal' life. B. H. Liddell Hart agrees, "Ensure that both plan and dispositions are flexible, adaptable to circumstances."

Don't get unnecessarily bumped and bruised along the way because you didn't create a plan. That is a surefire way to experience real failure. And no one wants to experience that or the feelings that go with it; so do some research, lay out a plan, show it to someone for feedback if that seems appropriate in your situation and then dive in with gusto!

Is This in Your Skillset?

Have you heard this before? "Everybody is a genius, but if you judge a fish by its ability to climb a tree, it will live its whole life believing that it is stupid." Is this thing that you seem to be failing at something that you are skilled at doing? Are you trying to be something that you are not? Or are not supposed to be? If so, you won't have the grace, the ability to do that thing well. If you are digging your heels in about it, you may need to ask yourself what is your reason for wanting to do this thing? Is this something that is deep in your heart to do or are you people pleasing? If it is in your heart to do, then do you need to get more training in an area? Do you need more practice? Can you find a mentor or do an internship? Are there videos that you can watch, podcasts to listen to, books to read, or classes to take?

There is a lot packed in that one paragraph. Take some time to think this through and make adjustments appropriate to your situation. Reach out to a trusted friend or counselor to talk about it. Many times "thinking out loud" is very helpful! Also, they may have a perspective that you are not seeing, could help you look at different angles, or provide direction and resources for you.

The Right Season - Timing

You have heard and will continue to hear me say, get after it, move it, go; and now I am going to ask you; is it the right timing for you to do this thing? The answer is different for everyone and this is its own deep subject so here are some points to consider:

Check your insides. Do you have a peace, a knowing, that even if things around you look not ready, the time to start planting the seeds for it is now? Are you experiencing failure or is it resistance? Sometimes resistance is your moxie being tested, but it can also be because now is not the time.

Moxie example: I had an injury that was so bad that I wasn't sure that I would walk normally again. After I was mostly better, I tried many times to work out within my abilities and found it hard. (I actually like working out so this was odd for me.) My muscles stayed tense, I couldn't go for long periods, etc and then I realized, I am scared. This has nothing to do with 'my body isn't ready to go at this again'; I was afraid to be reinjured and lose use of my leg again. Once I reconciled that, I took time to see myself completing a workout (within my current ability) and then I did it! My muscles still hurt and I couldn't go for very long at first, but everything about it was different that time and every time thereafter!

Timing example: I kept trying to go back to college and nothing worked. I felt like I should just back off, but I kept pressing, feeling like I was pushing against a wall that I should leave alone. Hard as I tried, I missed the application deadline anyway. Only two months later my life turned upside down and I realize that had I been in college, I would have had to drop out.

The lesson here is to pay attention to the other clues going on. What is in your control and what is not? What do you believe beyond a shadow of a doubt you should or should not do? Are you afraid or is there some real reason to pause? This does not mean that you will not miss it now and again, but you will have more "successes" than "failures" taking this approach.

If you still need help with this, continue to read through this book and then come back to this section. Some of your questions may be answered elsewhere. Remember you are an interwoven, not easily put in a single box, human.

The Historic Failure

This subject technically goes into the fear category that we overviewed in Chapter 2, but the answer for it could include any of the topics previously listed, so I saved it for last. Have you failed at this thing in the past so you don't want to get back on the horse and try again? Have you hit the ground so many times that you shudder at the idea of enduring that humiliation again? Do you find that you have a history of feeling like a failure so it is harder and harder to jump in and take chances?

Which subject that we have already gone over did that/those fall into? Are you regularly not planning? Self-sabotaging? Not doing research first or doing so much that you don't produce anything but another analysis? Are you sure it is something that you should be doing?

Once you find the root of your "always failing", make that adjustment/s and you will have a different outcome. Sometimes it is a combination of things, because the human is a complex creature. I suggest that you work backward looking at the sections of this chapter to see if you need a simple adjustment and then work your way back to Chapter 2 if you find that you are still not getting the desired results.

If you still need some direction, speak to a trusted friend or counselor, or message on the Discussion Group and we'll dive into it with you. If you have your answer, but you still don't want to get back in the boat, that is rooted in fear. Once you acknowledge that, read and consider these:

JUST BECAUSE YOU FAIL ONCE, DOESN'T MEAN YOU'RE GONNA FAIL AT EVERYTHING. KEEP TRYING, HOLD ON, AND ALWAYS, ALWAYS, ALWAYS BELIEVE IN YOURSELF, BECAUSE IF YOU DON'T, THEN WHO WILL, SWEETIE?
Marilyn Monroe

Failure is not falling down.
but refusing to get up.
Chinese Proverb

YOU DON'T DROWN BY FALLING IN THE WATER:
YOU DROWN BY STAYING THERE.
Edwin Louis Cole

Do not occupy yourself with regrets of
past mistakes or worries about the
present. Rather, be more occupied with
your visions for the future.
Eugene C. Onyibo

Please read that one again. "Do not occupy your-self with regrets of past mistakes." That will stop you cold at some point if you just focus on what a looser you (think you) are. Now is the time to take the reins of your life back. Make the necessary adjustments with confidence that the results can be different this time and can set you on a new, better course!

Thus far we have looked at the "negatives" of failure. We have seen how it is scary and has the ability to drum up deep seated and highly undesir-able emotions that can drive you to anything from *over*compensating to full paralysis and non-action. Hopefully by now you are starting to realize that failure doesn't have to be seen as the "looser" category that most put it in and often times what is being called a failure, actually isn't. Most of the time it is just something that happens along the way.

Let's move to Chapter 4 where we discuss perspectives and ways to make a perceived failure work for you.

Chapter Four

The more you fail and recover and improve, the better you are as a person. Ever meet someone who's always had everything work out for them with zero struggle? They usually have the depth of a puddle. Or they don't exist." ~ Chris Hardwick

I n this Chapter, we will look at the opposite end of the "failure" spectrum and Thomas Edison will introduce the concept. "I have not failed 10,000 times. I have not failed once. I have succeeded in proving that those 10,000 ways will not work. When I have eliminated the ways that will not work, I will find the way that will work." This is how to view a misstep, mistake, or anything considered less than an ideal outcome, in a "positive" way. Let's see what some of these benefits are and find ways to attract better experiences and a renewed view of the word failure. Let's examine why some people are excited by what could have otherwise shut them down.

Benefits of Continuing and Giving it Your Best Effort

Hal Elrod suggested in Chapter 5 of *The Miracle Equation* to set high goals and work them to the fullest understanding because even if you don't reach them, you're a better person and have more skills. My interpretation of the same idea comes from the 2006 movie *Facing the Giants* when I encourage people to and live by 'leaving it all on the field'. Do your very best, and give it all that you have, all the way to the end. The idea Hal, and the movie, and myself are trying to get across is that life is better when you make great effort. There is so much that comes along to enhance it and ways to take things to another level along with getting to live a better version of yourself. As you keep dusting off and going again, as you give 100% until the clock strikes 12, you grow into a better version of yourself.

- You will gain more confidence in your ability to push, push, push and even if it didn't turn out ideally, there is a sense of satisfaction and solidness that no pill, drink, or shopping spree can provide to you. It also comes with the motivation, and usually creativity and ideas to do it better the next time. If you allow it to be an exciting experience, instead of something you have to grind your way through, you will also have *that* thrill inside of you as well.

- You will have a life of few to no regrets when you take on that mindset. There is a security deep inside that settles you knowing that you could not have done anything else, more, or better because with what you had available to you, at that time, you gave it your best!

- You will become resilient, bouncing back faster and with fewer bruises each time you go at it. Things that may have crushed you five years ago barely tickle your attention today.

- Empathy will increase because you will be able to identify with others on more levels and in more situations. This will, in turn, make for better relationships and could create an increase of other good experiences in your life.

- Acceptance is another trait that you will become more adept at and will serve you all of the days of your life. You will use this powerful tool to keep your emotions out of the mix when faced with difficulty. This allows you to have a clearer head in the matter as well as keeping you out of the emotional storm that could take you down. It also adds to resilience.

- You will realize that the hamster wheel life isn't cutting it. You will want more and want to *be* more. I don't mean in an unsatisfied, hating life way, but it in a 'you know more can be accomplished and you are just the person to do it' way. The same ole is no longer attractive to you. You will seek out new opportunities and ways to use creativity, problem solving, and innovation.

These are just a few of the ways that you grow as

a person, deeper, and stronger, as you encounter and move past less than perfect outcomes. Many of them overlap so they feed each other, which continues to perpetuate your forward movement! In short, life can be exciting again!

Redefining the F Word

Previously, if it didn't go the way that you thought it should, you most likely defined the outcome as a failure. Now that you have seen more of the root and truth of it, choose more appropriate words to describe the situation. It increases your willingness to get back on the horse and also lightens up the mood around whatever it is that you are doing. I am not trying to be flippant, but am using simple ideas to explain complex topics. Yes, this works even in a business venture, saving your marriage, and recreating your life after it was destroyed. Go at it with an excitement and gusto, or at least a hopeful mindset instead of mild dread of a bad outcome. That in itself starts you out on better footing. So when asked, you are:

- Learning
- In the process of understanding

- Figuring it out
- Gaining experience
- Experimenting
- On a quest or adventure
- Investigating
- Practicing
- Trying something new to see what happens

All of these terms and more are appropriate to describe why you didn't get it perfectly your first time around. Basically you are saying that you have gained some insight and are ready to go at it again. However you phrase it, choose an uplifting and affirming way of describing your experience.

Another Perspective

Napoleon Hill pointed out that "many successful people have found opportunities in failure and adversity that they could not recognize in more favorable circumstances." Sometimes it is seeing the thing gone wrong that sparks a revelation of a better way of doing something, and sharpens your senses to alternative routes. Lean in when things go wrong and employ the failure analysis. You can come away with more knowledge and insight!

Celebrate Every Victory

Society likes to celebrate the finish line. However, we are inspired by the 'how they got there' stories; the sacrifices, early mornings, dedication, etc. Those are worth noting! Celebrate your victories, big *and* small. Do not discount what went right just because it was little. Highlight those things and build on them! Some people who have been there, done that agree:

Small victories are better than none.
Neal Shusterman

Small wins are essential, not just for the victories themselves, but because they give you more energy, self-confidence, and enthusiasm.
Lynda Gratton

Don't wait until you have reached your goal to be proud of yourself. Be proud of every step you take toward reaching your goal.
Unknown

Keep Your Plan in Front of You

Some people say to keep your eye on the prize. While that statement has merit, I believe that if you have a plan that takes you to the prize, looking at the plan keeps  you on the path to it because you are diligently working toward the prize by using the plan.

If you are just staring at your finish line, it could look far away at times and get discouraging. But if you are just looking one or two steps ahead at your plan, you are always on target! If you stumble, you don't see your finish line fade, you simply look at your plan and get back onto the correct step and keep moving. As my sister regularly says, "Take the next right step". As you do, you will make your way to your goal and greatly reduce a true or perceived failure. (The need for a plan has been previously discussed. If you don't have a plan, make one today.)

Mark Esper's advise is both encouraging and uplifting: "Stay focused on your mission, remain steadfast in your pursuit of excellence, and always do the right thing." I believe that we can all benefit from these sound words.

Be the Bendy Tree

When storms come, usually it is the tree that bends with the wind that survives. While there are some exceptions and there may still be leaves scattered and branches down, more times than not, it is the rigid, refusing to budge trees that find themselves toppled over during a storm. When the winds come, bend some, find a different way to accomplish it. As Sissy Gavrilaki puts it, "Failure is nothing more than a chance to revise your strategy." I once heard it said to keep the goal the same, but be flexible in your approach. Flexibility will serve you well!

It's Not Just You

Just by the sheer volume of books, songs, and movies on the subject, hopefully you realize that it isn't just you that has had a setback. However, if this thought plagues you, consider a mentor, support group, counselor, educating yourself on the subject that you feel you are floundering in, or reach out for help in a way that works for you. Don't get stuck in the "poor me" cycle. Some of the best have fallen hard, yet they get back up. Let Nelson Mandela drive this home, then set up your life so that you can say the same: "Do not judge me by my successes, judge me by how many times I fell down and got back up again." So if you have found yourself in a less than perfect situation and decided to keep going, you have found yourself in quality company.

Be Careful What You Tie In

John Sinclair said, "Failure is a bruise, not a tattoo." I'd also like to add that it isn't part of your name or a title that you go by. Don't tie

your self worth into your successes *or* failures. Here's another simple, but highly effective example. When I was a young mommy, a lady heard me exclaim to my son "good boy" as I clapped my hands cheering his efforts to crawl toward me. She kindly encouraged me to *never equate his value to his actions.* Maybe it was how gently she presented it or simply because it was such a profound thought, but whatever it was, I took her suggestion to heart and applied it not only to raising my son, but started applying it to myself as well. I learned that I had a lot of "untying" to do for myself and I didn't want him to have to go through that. Right away I could be heard saying, "great job", "well done", and "awesome", but never again "good boy".

Like Minded People

Surround yourself with like-minded people and those that stretch you. As Warren Buffet put it, "It's better to hang out with people better than you. Pick out associates whose behavior is better than yours, and you'll drift in that direction."

When my son was in junior high, sometimes the neighborhood high school boys would let him play basketball with them. Even though each time was a struggle, he realized when he played with his junior high friends that he was becoming better than them. Why? Because always working harder to play with the big kids challenged him to bring his best game so when he was against people who didn't do that, he naturally rose to the top. Make sure that your friends are the kind of people that you want to be like and maybe even a bit better. Have lunch with the co-workers that you can identify with, but might also be going places you would like to. If you participate in sports or hobbies, gather with those who share your interest and can bring something for you to learn to the table. As it has been said, "If you are the smartest person in the room, you are in the wrong room".

Sometimes you cannot hang out with people that are of like mind *and* smarter than you. Partake of what you have access to, then look elsewhere for the missing part. Do you have friends, coworkers, etc that are likeminded and encouraging, but you are all on the same level? Then level up by listening to podcasts, taking a class, reading a book, finding a Meet Up, or online group to take you to another level in a specific area.

Move It

One of my most favorite quotes is by Kenneth Hagin, Sr, "You cannot steer a  parked car." Once you have learned about the subject, flip fear off and get moving. This does not guarantee that there will not be a hiccup, but it does guarantee that the journey has begun, thus the learning and adventure! Will Rodgers and Johann Wolfgang Von Goethe agree with me. Will said, "Even if you're on the right track, you'll get run over if you just sit there." And Von Goethe, in his inspirational style said, "Whatever you can do, or dream you can, begin it. Boldness has genius, magic, and power in it." So, let's get going!

Be Bold and Courageous

"There is no failure for the man who realizes his power, who never knows when he is beaten; there is no failure for the determined endeavor; the unconquerable will. There is no failure for the man who gets up every time he falls, who rebounds like a rubber ball, who persists when everyone else gives up, who pushes on when everyone else turns back." – Orison Sweet Marden

---

There is no substance or device that can make you bold or courageous. It is simply a choice of will. You come to a point where standing up, stepping up, not budging, and the like are what you live by. It isn't easy to fall in front of people, to try and get a face full of "nope". That's why few keep on. But the bold and courageous will live a life that the majority never will.

There are small libraries of books and hundreds of quotes on boldness and courage. It is hard to narrow it down to just a few great ones, but these regularly speak to me so hopefully they can get you started as well.

> I'd rather attempt to do something great and fail than to attempt to do nothing and succeed.
> Robert H. Schuller

> You must do the thing you think you cannot do.
> Eleanor Roosevelt

> It's only after you've stepped outside your comfort zone that you begin to change, grow, and transform.
> Roy T. Bennet

> Be willing to take a chance, because you never know how perfect something could turn out to be.
> Unknown

Find a bold/courage quote that works for you and stick it wherever you most need to see it. And when it is time to face that thing that has you shaking from head to toe, chest up to it, and watch life provide mountaintop views you have never dreamed of!

Focus on What is in Your Control

There are some things in your control and some things that are not. As you learned in "Be a Bendy Tree", sometimes you need to adapt to the situation and focus on what you *can* do. Time will be passing anyway and you will be expending energy anyway, so make it count.

I needed the approval on a project so the next big step could be taken. While I waited for the approval to come in, I did all of the little things that would also need to be done at some point in the project that weren't directly related to the approval. Once I received the green light, I had not lost any momentum and continued on with the project. I could have sat there twiddling my thumbs annoyed that I had to wait around to go to the next step. Instead, I found a way to continue moving the project forward remaining productive and not at all disturbed. If you feel like you have been stopped or have to wait on something, what *can* you do? I could not write this section without putting these two quotes in. They are simple yet just what you might need at some point.

Start where you are.
Use what you have.
Do what you can.
Arthur Ashe

At the end of the day, you can't control the results; you can only control your effort level and your focus.
Ben Zobrist

Don't Give Up

I have a small folder that I have added to over the years. It is simply titled *ICE*, which means "In Case of Emergency". I keep it close by and have had to use it a few times in the last decade when I was tempted to throw up my hands and give up. In the folder is various clippings and pictures and reminders of why I am doing what I do and that quitting isn't an option. The items in that folder encourage, motivate, and remind me. I do have my vision all around me, but that small folder, at a handful of insanely trying times, has been pulled off of the shelf and carried over to my bed where I have poured through it, regaining my "umph" to not throw in the towel. I just wanted you to know that everyone has those crossroad moments. I think that the only subject there are more quotes on than courage is that of not giving up, which, by default, does require a level of courage. Here are three that really stand out.

Fear regret more than failure.
Taryn Rose

IF YOU'RE TIRED OF STARTING OVER,
STOP GIVING UP.
Shia LaBeouf

Our greatest weakness lies in giving up. The most certain way to succeed is always to try just one more time.
Thomas A. Edison

One thing to keep in mind about quitting is that it isn't just in the big things after everything has come crashing down, gone wrong, shriveled up, and essentially your life looks like the great battle aftermath of a World War 3 movie. You can give up when you've had a long day and instead of going to the gym like you promised yourself, your workout is comprised of how quickly you can sprint to your recliner before you plop into it, and alternating fingers on the remote control so that they all get equal exertion. Technically this can fall under the heading of dedication, motivation, will power, self-discipline, etc, but it works just as well here. If you set a specific health goal for yourself, and your plan to attain that goal says that tonight is gym night, you are choosing to fail in that area when you choose to quit on your plan that night. This idea can quickly spin out of the scope of this book, but I wanted to at least present the general idea for your consideration.

There you have it! A few more ways to view, consider, and avoid failure, further empowering *you* to control your attitude, actions, and life! Let's head over to Chapter 5 and wrap up.

Chapter Five

Sticking to good habits can be hard work, and mistakes are part of the process. Don't declare failure. Instead, use your mistakes as opportunities to grow stronger and become better. ~ Amy Morin

Well, here we are, near the end of another workshop book! In the beginning we asked a lot of questions about failure. Can you now answer these questions about "failure"?

Is it good or is it bad?

Do we embrace it or shun it?

Is there a middle ground?

Who do we listen to?

What is the right answer?

This book promised to "teach you how place "failure" where it belongs, on your terms, so that you are equipped to move forward." Now that you have the tools at your disposal, what is your next step or steps? Did you pause at sections that applied to you and make the necessary corrections? Were you able to investigate anything that you have questions about? How have you grown? Take some time to consider and answer these questions. Don't rush away from the book. Make sure that you got what you came for.

By now you should be able to see that many things that have been defined as failure are actually not at all a failure, that even if something was a failure that you can still use it for your good, and that there are ways to minimize the chances of failure. Hopefully things are clearer for you and you have been able to look at your life and see places that can be adjusted to allow you more control and peace over perceptions of things gone wrong.

I encourage you to make use of the resources listed on MsJoysPlace.com for this and other books, to take your healing and growth up a notch, and I would equally encourage you to take things to another level by joining the Discussion Group at www.facebook.com/groups/msjoysplace. You can also get there by clicking the "Join the Discussion" link at the bottom of my website. Don't do life alone. *We would love to include you in our like-mind group!*

With that said, let's wrap up our time together by tuning back in to the Toastmaster's meeting...

Every person at the meeting that night wrote down, to the point of asking her to repeat it so that we got it right, what JR ended her speech with: "Failure doesn't have to be final. Messes can be redeemed. And I can be free to try and fail and try again."

However you have decided to apply what you have encountered in these pages, remember what JR said. Whatever way you choose to phrase it, the meaning is true for us too!

Bibliography

Duplantis, J. (2016). *The everyday visionary: Focus your thoughts, change your life*. Touchstone Books.

Failure analysis. Failure Analysis - an overview | ScienceDirect Topics. (n.d.). Retrieved February 15, 2023, from https://www.sciencedirect.com/topics/engineering/failure-analysis

Failure is not a disgrace if you have sincerely done your best. Napoleon Hill Foundation. (2021, October 31). Retrieved February 15, 2023, from https://www.naphill.org/tftd/thought_for_the_day_12-13-21/

Many successful people have found opportunities in failure and adversity that they could not recognize in more favorable circumstances. Napoleon Hill Foundation. (2021, October 31). Retrieved February 15, 2023, from https://www.naphill.org/tftd/thought_for_the_day_11-10-21/

Things That Will Happen When You Finally Decide to Live Your Dreams. (n.d.). Retrieved from https://www.linkedin.com/pulse/31-things-happen-when-you-finally-decide-live-your-dreams-hardy-1/.

What is a failure analysis? - definition from Corrosionpedia. Corrosionpedia. (n.d.). Retrieved February 15, 2023, from https://www.corrosionpedia.com/definition/487/failure-analysis

What is failure analysis? definition and examples. Market Business News. (2018, August 7). Retrieved February 15, 2023, from https://marketbusinessnews.com/financial-glossary/failure-analysis/

About the Author

Joy has always felt a strong calling to help others, leading her to volunteer in various capacities including mentoring, which she done for more than 20 years. During that time, she has helped people from all walks of life and ages face and overcome the darkest moments of their lives as well as those who have huge dreams that they were unable to achieve because of life's hard knocks. Joy has carried on her work as a mentor with great enthusiasm and love, creating strong bonds with many of them. As the years progressed Joy began to understand how much strength is needed to face the challenges with which life tests us, often finding us unprepared, and realizing how important it is to take small steps to solve any problem and achieve lasting results.

In addition to her work as a mentor, Joy has a love for writing and has trained those skills by ghostwriting and copy editing for over 20 years. Finally combining her two passions, Joy is now sharing her experiences in dealing with personal growth and overcoming the odds through her books that are designed as short reads that are easy to understand, and with the intention of removing the obstacle of the struggle of starting, which aids in continuing her readers' journey of growth.

She also offers a private discussion group for her readers to share, celebrate and encourage one another. Come join the community!

Join the Discussion!

facebook.com/groups/msjoysplace

MsJoysPlace.com
Resources, Articles,
Links, and More!

Other Social Media
@MsJoysPlace

email:
hello@msjoysplace.com

www.ingramcontent.com/pod-product-compliance
Lightning Source LLC
Chambersburg PA
CBHW030507130626
46549CB00007B/2878